BBC earth

DO YOU KNOW?

Level 1

ANIMALS AND THEIR BODIES

Inspired by BBC Earth TV series and developed with input from BBC Earth natural history specialists

Written by Ruth A. Musgrave
Text adapted by Jennifer Dobson
Series Editor: Nick Coates

LADYBIRD BOOKS

UK | USA | Canada | Ireland | Australia
India | New Zealand | South Africa

Ladybird Books is part of the Penguin Random House group of companies
whose addresses can be found at global.penguinrandomhouse.com.
www.penguin.co.uk   www.puffin.co.uk   www.ladybird.co.uk

Penguin
Random House
UK

First published 2020
001

Printed in China

A CIP catalogue record for this book is available from the British Library

ISBN: 978–0–241–35583–1

All correspondence to:
Ladybird Books Ltd
Penguin Random House Children's
One Embassy Gardens, New Union Square,
5 Nine Elms Lane, London SW8 5DA

Contents

New words

frighten

fur

hold
(verb)

insect

jump
(verb)

plant
(noun)

same

smell
(verb)

tail

tongue

tooth
(teeth)

wing

Are people and animals the same?

People need food and water.
So do animals.

People have ears, eyes and noses.
So do animals.

Some animals have
wings and **tails**.
People do not.

This Arctic fox finds food with its ears, eyes and nose.

A tiger drinks water.

A fish swims with its tail.

LOOK!

Look at the pages.
How are these animals the same as you?
How are these animals different from you?

How many ears do animals have?

Animals can hear with their ears.

Some animals have big ears.

Some animals have small ears.

People have two ears.
Some animals
have one ear.

ear

A praying mantis
has one ear.

This cricket has
ears on its legs.

THINK!

What sounds can you hear now?

How do animals see?

Most animals have eyes. They can look for food.

This humpback whale can see under the water.

Some animals have big eyes. They can see at night.

An aye-aye has big eyes to see at night.

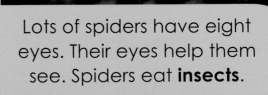

Lots of spiders have eight eyes. Their eyes help them see. Spiders eat **insects**.

THINK!

Aye-ayes have very big eyes.
Are your eyes big or small?
Which animal has very small eyes?

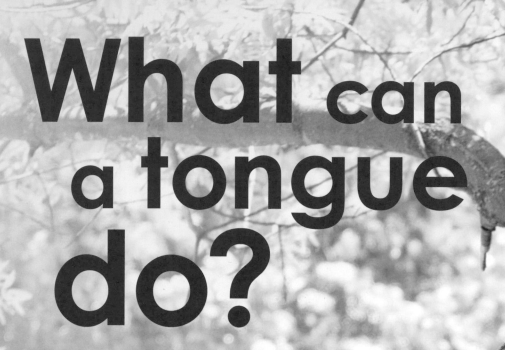

What can a tongue do?

Some animals find food with their **tongues**.

A giraffe's tongue gets leaves.

An anteater eats insects with its long tongue.

A Komodo dragon **smells** with its tongue.

▶ WATCH!

Watch the video (see page 32).
Which body parts help an anteater to get food?

What do animals eat?

Some animals eat **plants**.

Some animals eat other animals.

A green sea turtle eats seagrass.

A pika eats flowers.

A cheetah eats animals.

A chameleon eats insects.

LOOK!

Look at the pages.
What does a chameleon eat?

Do animals have big teeth?

Teeth help animals to eat.

Big teeth can **frighten** other animals, too.

A caiman catches food with its teeth.

This fish **holds** food with its teeth.

This chimpanzee frightens animals with its teeth.

This lion has big teeth.

 FIND OUT!

Use books or the internet to find three other animals that have big teeth.

Which animal has a long nose?

An elephant has got a trunk. A trunk is a very long nose.

An elephant holds things with its trunk.

An elephant smells with its trunk, too.

THINK!

Elephants hold things with their trunks.
What body parts can you use to hold things?

What has lots of legs and feet?

Insects have six legs.
Some animals have more legs.

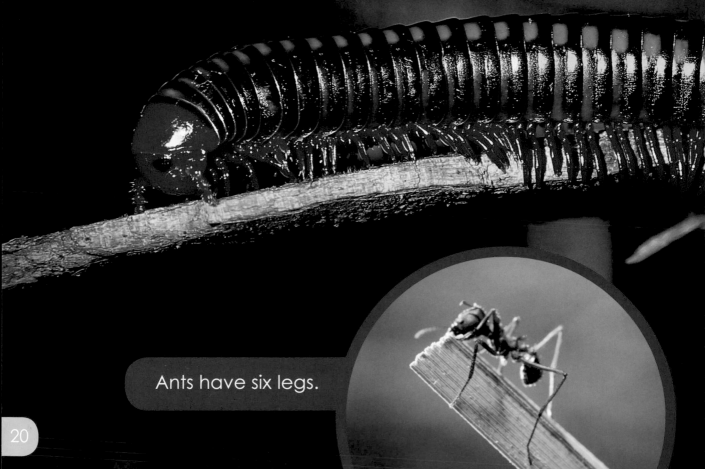

Ants have six legs.

A sea star has lots of feet. It does not swim. It walks.

This millipede has lots of legs.

PROJECT

Work in a group.
Invent your own animal. How many ears, eyes, arms, legs or wings does it have? How does it use the parts of its body? Draw a picture of your animal. Give it a name.

What can animals do with their tails?

Animals can do a lot with their tails.

This harvest mouse holds grass with its tail.

A fish swims with its tail.

A seahorse holds on to things with its tail.

▶ WATCH!

Watch the video (see page 32).
What does the mouse do with its tail?
What wants to eat the mouse?

Why do animals fly?

Birds, bats and insects can fly. They can find food, friends and homes.

Bats and birds have two wings.

This dragonfly has four wings.

This bird flies and catches insects.

THINK!

Imagine you can fly. Where would you go? What would you do?

Can fish fly?

Flying fish cannot fly.
They **jump**.

These flying
fish jump out
of the water.

They go back in the water and swim.

A flying fish swims with its tail.

▶ WATCH!

Watch the video (see page 32).
What helps the fish to jump?

Are all monkeys the same?

All monkeys have two eyes, a nose and a mouth.

But monkeys are not all the **same**.

This monkey's **fur** has lots of colours.

This monkey has a blue face and a red nose.

This monkey has long fur.

 PROJECT

Work in a group.
Find out where monkeys live in the world.
Do you live near monkeys?

Quiz

Choose the correct answers.

1 An anteater eats insects with its . . .
a tongue.
b ears.

2 A caiman catches food with its . . .
a nose.
b teeth.

3 An elephant's long nose is a . . .
a tail.
b trunk.

4 A sea star . . .
  a walks.
  b swims.

5 A flying fish can . . .
  a fly.
  b jump.

Visit www.ladybirdeducation.co.uk for
FREE DO YOU KNOW? teaching resources.

- video clips with simplified voiceover and subtitles
- video and comprehension activities
- class projects and lesson plans
- audio recording of every book
- digital version of every book
- full answer keys

To access video clips, audio tracks and digital books:

1 Go to **www.ladybirdeducation.co.uk**
2 Click "Unlock book"
3 Enter the code below

OulB6pe00P

Stay safe online! Some of the DO YOU KNOW? activities ask children to do extra research online. Remember:

- ensure an adult is supervising;
- use established search engines such as Google or Kiddle;
- children should never share personal details, such as name, home or school address, telephone number or photos.